Peace of
Mind®

Peace of Mind
Flex Curriculum

Grade 4

Fifteen engaging, flexible and experiential lessons that equip students with the skills to manage big emotions, learn empathy and compassion, build healthy relationships, and express emotions in American Sign Language.

Linda Ryden
Including original stories, illustrations and videos

Welcome to the Peace of Mind Community!

Peace of
Mind®

Questions? Comments?
We'd love to hear from you!

Please visit teachpeaceofmind.org or
contact us at info@TeachPeaceofMind.org.

Peace of Mind Publications

Curriculum

Peace of Mind Core Curriculum for Early Childhood

Peace of Mind Core Curriculum for Grades 1 & 2

Peace of Mind Core Curriculum for Grade 3

Peace of Mind Core Curriculum for Grades 4 & 5

Peace of Mind Core Curriculum for Middle School

Peace of Mind Flex Curriculum for Kindergarten

Peace of Mind Flex Curriculum for Grades 1 & 2

Peace of Mind Flex Curriculum for Grade 3

Peace of Mind Flex Curriculum for Grade 4

Peace of Mind Flex Curriculum for Grades 5-8

Social Justice Lesson Curriculum for Grades 3-5

Storybooks

Henry is Kind

Rosie's Brain / El Cerebro de Rosita

Marleigh is Mindful / Marleigh practica la conciencia plena

Marleigh's Big Feelings

Mason and the Conflict CAT / Mason y el conflicto CAT

Quinn and the Worry Channel

Sergio Sees the Good

Tyaja Uses the Think Test

TeachPeaceofMind.org

Peace of Mind Inc. Washington DC 20015

https://TeachPeaceofMind.org

Copyright 2025 Linda Ryden and Peace of Mind Inc.

Editor: Cheryl Cole Dodwell

Cover and Interior Design: Schwa Design Group

Illustrations, Graphics and Videos: Linda Ryden

Logo: Pittny Creative

ISBN: 979-8-9998662-2-6

LCCN: 2025917681

Published 2025

Peace of Mind Flex Curriculum For Grade 4

Peace of Mind Flex At-a-Glance

Lesson	Topic	Mindfulness Practice and ASL	Materials Needed
All lessons require a way to show a short video to the class and your Kindness Pal list. Worksheets and Coloring Sheets are included with the lessons.			
1.	Introduction to Mindfulness and Kindness Pals	Four Square Breathing ASL: Happy	Four Square Breathing Coloring Sheet
2	Take Five Breathing	Four Square Breathing and Take Five Breathing ASL: Sad	Take Five Breathing Coloring Sheet and Worksheet
3	Gravity Hands	Take Five Breathing and Gravity Hands ASL: Angry	Gravity Hands Coloring Sheet
4	Flower Breathing	Gravity Hands and Flower Breathing ASL: Scared	Flower Breath Coloring Sheet
5	Visualization	Flower Breathing and Visualization ASL: Silly	Visualization Worksheet and Coloring Sheet
6	Make up Your own Breath	Mindfulness Helper Choice ASL: Surprised	Create your Own Breath Worksheet
7	Sergio Sees the Good	ASL: Surprise Mindfulness Helper Choice ASL: I Feel	Paper Cups, small objects.
8	Tell Me Something Good	Mindfulness Helper Choice ASL: Frustrated	Ten Little Good Things Worksheet.
9	Rosie's Brain	Mindfulness Helper Choice ASL: Excited	Brain Poster Copies
10	Mason and the Conflict CAT	Candle Breathing ASL: How are you feeling today?	Candle Breathing Coloring Sheet
11	Conflict CAT Role Play	Mindfulness Helper Choice ASL: Hungry	Conflict CAT Poster
12	Quinn and the Worry Channel	Mindfulness Helper Choice ASL: Thirsty	Remote Control Breathing Coloring Sheet
13	Tyaja Uses the THINK Test	Mindfulness Helper Choice ASL: Peaceful	Think Test Coloring Sheet
14	THiNK Test Role Plays	Mindfulness Helper Choice ASL: Worried	
15	Kindness Taps	Heartfulness ASL: Loved	Heartfulness Coloring Sheet

Introduction to the Peace of Mind Peace of Mind Flex Curriculum

Welcome to the Peace of Mind Flex Curriculum! If you are looking for a series of flexible mindfulness-based SEL lessons that can be used daily or weekly, this curriculum is for you! This Flex Curriculum is designed to be used in schools and out-of-school time programs where time or staffing constraints allow only 15-20 minutes for social and emotional learning lessons. Lessons may be broken up into modules and taught over the course of a week.

Curriculum Theory of Change

Our Theory of Change (ToC) is the same for both our Flex Curriculum and our Core Curriculum. The ToC includes our Curriculum Pillars, Learning Experiences, Core Teaching Practices, and the Outcomes we hope to see for students. Here it is:

Pillars

The Flex Curriculum is built on Peace of Mind's 6 foundational pillars: Mindfulness, Brain Science, Kindness and Compassion, Gratitude, Conflict Resolution and Social Justice. Engaging and fun, this series uses animated stories and mindfulness practice videos along with interactive discussions and activities to engage students in:

- experiencing mindfulness practice for themselves;
- learning what happens in their brains when they experience a big emotion;
- learning how mindful practices can affect their ability to respond;
- learning how mindfulness can help in resolving conflicts peacefully.

Every lesson ends with Kindness Pals, a pair practice that helps students get to know each other and build a caring classroom community in a relatively short time.

Learning Experiences

This Flex Curriculum, like our Core Curriculum, is designed to promote learning experiences that center student well-being and agency while supporting a kind and inclusive classroom and school community. You'll notice that students learn mindfulness not only for themselves, but for their relationships with others. The curriculum is experiential and inclusive with opportunities for student leadership and personal growth throughout. Schools that use Peace of Mind year-after-year in all grade levels will find consistent themes with age-appropriate lessons. Peace of Mind also helps school communities to develop a common language and skill set related to our own well-being, building healthy relationships, and solving conflicts peacefully.

Outcomes

When taught with fidelity, The Peace of Mind Flex Curriculum will help students to:

- increase their self-awareness and self-regulation;
- understand the basic science related to their emotions;
- regularly practice kindness, compassion and gratitude;
- be more aware of and more skillfully focus their thoughts;
- build positive relationships with peers and adults;
- build kind and inclusive classrooms.

Core Teaching Practices

Through our work with partner schools and academic researchers, we have identified five core teaching practices for effective, impactful implementation of Peace of Mind.

1. **Follow the Scope and Sequence of the Curriculum**

   This lesson sequence is designed to first give students a foundational set of mindfulness practices to help them manage their emotions and learn to put space between their reactions to a big feeling and their response. Gratitude practice follows and an introduction to one aspect of how our brains work: our negativity bias. Students learn more basic brain science in the lesson on Rosie's Brain. The curriculum, like every lesson, closes with kindness practice. With this foundation, students are ready for the conflict resolution lessons.

   - **Mindfulness**
     In all lessons, students learn and practice mindfulness exercises,

building their own tool kit to help them notice and manage big emotions. Students experience the effects of each practice personally and begin to discern which practices are most helpful to them.

- **Gratitude**
  We explore gratitude in several different ways including our brain's tendency to focus on the negative and how gratitude practice helps to balance this tendency by focusing on small good things we experience. Through stories, games and activities, students experience this for themselves.

- **Brain Science**
  Through the Rosie's Brain story, students gain powerful insight into what happens in our brains when we get angry and why mindfulness helps us calm down.

- **Conflict Resolution**
  Building on the foundation laid in earlier lessons, students learn to use mindfulness and a new understanding of their brains to understand when they are in a conflict and how they can use their skills to calm down, apologize and work out a peaceful solution.

- **Kindness and Compassion**
  We end the curriculum with a focus on self-compassion and compassion for others, trying out Kindness Taps as a final way of connecting with and appreciating each other.

- **Social Justice**
  Former U.S. Surgeon General Vivek Murthy said that "mental health is the defining public health crisis of our time." The ultimate goal of the Peace of Mind Program is to create a kinder, more peaceful world with and for our children. We begin by helping to create classroom communities where students feel loved and seen. We help children and their grownups learn how to recognize and manage their emotions, how to feel compassion for others and themselves and how to work out conflicts peacefully. We hope that with these personal and interpersonal skills, children will grow up to find peaceful solutions to the most challenging social justice issues of our time.

2. **Practice Trauma Sensitive Teaching**

   All lessons include three important components of trauma-sensitive teaching:

   - **Invitational** - Mindfulness practice is always invitational. While we expect everyone to sit together during the mindful moments, we invite students to choose whether or not to engage with a practice. They can choose for themselves, but they cannot interfere with someone else's choice. We ask everyone to be respectful of others while making their own decision about whether to do a practice or not. Students are welcome to just sit quietly.

- **Student-centered** - We teach mindfulness practices for students' own well-being. We teach a variety of practices not so students can master them all, but so they can find the ones that work best for them. If a student is having a hard time with a practice, suggest that they choose another one that works better for them.

- **Flexible** - We don't require students to close their eyes or sit in a certain way to practice. If students need to make modifications to a practice (keeping their eyes open or walking quietly in the back of the room, for example) to help themselves feel comfortable, this is fine as long as their choices do not interfere with others' comfort and safety.

3. Use Strength-Based Approaches

You will notice that the scripts offered for the lessons use strength-based language: language that focuses on students' abilities, interests and potential, not deficits. The curriculum is designed to promote student agency and leadership, especially through the role of Mindfulness Helper. The Mindfulness Helper is a student who leads the class in the mindfulness practice for the day. Here's how it works:

- The teacher consults their alphabetical roll list and chooses a student to be the Mindfulness Helper (MH) for the day.

- The teacher encourages the class to offer sign language applause for the person who is chosen that day.

- The MH can sit near the teacher.

- With the teacher's help the MH says slowly, "Let's get into our mindful bodies…. Let's close our eyes or look down. … Let's Invite three deep breaths." Always offer the students a choice about keeping their eyes open or closed. At this point the teacher or student will lead the rest of the mindfulness practice as instructed in the lesson.

- The MH rings the bell/chime when the mindfulness practice is complete.

- The teacher then asks the MH to return to their seat.

Repeating the same words each class is important to help students develop a routine to help them begin to practice on their own.

4. **Model What You Teach**

   We know from research and our own experience that modeling what we are teaching is one of the most effective ways of engaging our students in mindfulness practice themselves. Students take their cues from you. You don't have to be an expert in mindfulness, but it is important to model using the practices yourself.

5. **Bring Yourself to the Curriculum**

   Once you are comfortable with the first four core teaching practices, we hope you will be able to bring yourself to the curriculum. If the script isn't quite how you would say things, please adapt so you feel comfortable. If you enjoy singing, bring that in! If you enjoy crafts, make that a part of what you do. If puppets are your thing, they're welcome!

Setting Expectations

The *Peace of Mind* curriculum plants seeds of mindfulness and compassion. These seeds grow and mature inside a student's mind and heart, positively affecting the way a person sees the world and operates within it. For some students, the outward positive effects are manifested quickly and clearly. For other students, it may take more time, and the outward signs of change may be subtle. All that we expect of students is to try to practice the skills in this curriculum as often as they can —just to try.

Some students have a much easier time sitting quietly than others. Keep your expectations reasonable. Sometimes a student who is sitting with their eyes wide open, legs jiggling, and fiddling with a pencil—but not talking—during mindfulness practice is doing their very best and is benefiting greatly from the effort. That's okay. The exercises in this curriculum are for the benefit of the children and, as long as they are not preventing other children from practicing, a little wiggling around is okay.

Try to put the guidelines in positive language such as "As long as you follow the directions you can continue to play the game." This can be much more effective than the more traditional way of saying, "If you don't follow the rules you can't play." Many children react negatively to orders like that but are perfectly happy to follow the rules when they are stated in a more neutral way.

Materials Needed

Lesson Slides. Accessible through this QR code:

- **Storybooks**

  Rosie's Brain, Sergio Sees the Good, Quinn and the Worry Channel, Tyaja Uses the THINK Test, and *Mason and the Conflict CAT* either in print copies or video read-alouds (links included in lessons and in slides - see QR code above.)

- **Worksheet and Coloring Sheet Copies**

  You will find related coloring sheets and worksheets right after each lesson. Please print what you need for your class. See "At-A-Glance" to easily find what you need for each lesson.

  Here's an idea! Send coloring sheets home after each class so that parents know what their children are learning in Peace Class. Or, turn the Coloring Sheets into a book for your students to Invite home at the end of the session!

- **Chime (optional)**

American Sign Language

A new addition to the Peace of Mind Curriculum, American Sign Language is a wonderful tool to use to help all children, regardless of English proficiency, learn about, explore and communicate their emotions. These lessons offer a very basic, simple introduction to expressing emotions in American Sign Language. The ASL included in these lessons is just an introduction to a rich language that can be used to communicate with students who are deaf and hard of hearing or who have other communication challenges.

For more information about learning ASL please visit:
www.nad.org/resources/american-sign-language/
learning-american-sign-language

A Note on Kindness Pals

Kindness Pals is an engaging and powerful activity that takes place every class period. Kindness Pal practice reminds children to make kindness part of their daily lives. Doing kind things for their Kindness Pals spills over into their treatment of others and so they can develop the habit of treating people with kindness through regular practice. Kindness Pals also gives children opportunities to get to know each other and to connect with others whom they might not have gotten along with in the past or whom they think they just don't like. Here's a quick video introduction to Kindness Pals.

Here is how it works:

- For each class, assign each student one Kindness Pal. You can pair up children in advance to ensure there aren't any repeated partnerships.

- When each child hears their Kindness Pal's name, emphasize that both pals, or the whole class, must say "Okay." **This is very important.** This response lets the teacher know that they have heard their assignment and that they know who their Kindness Pal is. Please practice this routine with your class. (**Watch this** video of kids doing Kindness pals.)

- Please let the class know that this is not a time for them to let the teacher or the class know how they feel about having that Kindness Pal. This avoids hurt feelings and also offers multiple chances to remind the children that they have the power to be kind and the power to hurt people's feelings. It all depends on their choices. This is a powerful lesson.

- Explain to the students that they will each receive one Kindness Pal each class period (or each week if you choose). Kindness Pals will participate in an activity together during the class period.

- You may also invite the students to do small kind things for their assigned Kindness Pals before the next class. Some examples of kind behavior might be to get a Pal's snack, stack their chair, or play together at recess. The following class, allow a few minutes for children to talk about what they did for their Pal.

- Optional: Use some sort of Talking Object (a stuffed animal or squishy ball) for the sharing. Toss the object to the first speaker and remind everyone that the person holding the object gets to talk and the rest of us get to listen.

- Kindness Pals sharing time is a perfect time to practice mindful listening. It's important to demonstrate how we listen mindfully with our whole bodies. You might even want to let a student lead the sharing.

- Assign new pals at the end of each class (or week).

Lesson 1
Introduction to Mindfulness, Kindness Pals and ASL

Slides: 1-12

1. Welcome to Peace of Mind!

You might say: *We're going to be learning about something called mindfulness. Have you ever heard of mindfulness before? What do you think it means?* **Invite some answers.**

Mindfulness means to pay attention, and we can pay attention to many different things. Mindfulness can also be about using our breath to help us take care of ourselves. How do you breathe when you run around for a long time? How do you breathe when you are scared? How do you breathe when you are nervous?

Today we are going to watch a video about a girl named Marleigh who we will be getting to know in Peace of Mind Class. She's a really good dancer, but she gets nervous when she has to perform in front of an audience. Do you ever get nervous? Let's see what Marleigh does when she gets nervous.

2. Mindful Moment

Show Marleigh Four Square Video. Marleigh introduces mindfulness and teaches the first practice.

Try Four Square Breathing with the class. **Try** taking 3 breaths this way.

Discuss: *Does breathing this way make you feel any different? Is it hard to hold your breath? Can you do it gently? Why do you think Four Square Breathing helped Marleigh feel less nervous about her performance? How do you feel?*

3. American Sign Language (ASL)

We're going to be learning a new way to share our feelings with each other called American Sign Language or ASL. ASL is a visual language - a language that we see with our eyes instead of listening to with our ears.

When we use ASL, we use our facial expressions, hand signals and body movements instead of saying words with our voices. Most of the people who use ASL are deaf (which means that they cannot hear with their ears) or hard of hearing which means they have trouble hearing with their ears. But lots of other people use it too. Once we learn how to share our feelings in ASL we'll start using it to share our feelings with each other.

We're going to start out by learning how to say "happy."
How do you feel in your body when you are happy?

Choose a few volunteers to demonstrate what "happy" looks like.

Let's watch a video of one of the Peace of Mind students showing us how to sign "happy." **Happy Video (the video is in the slides)**

4. Kindness Pals

Introduce Kindness Pals. You might say: *Now we're going to do something fun called Kindness Pals. Every class we're going to get a new Kindness Pal. Your Kindness Pal is somebody that you will get to know a little bit better. You get to do kind things for them, and they get to do kind things for you. Then, next time you'll get a new Kindness Pal. There's one important rule of Kindness Pals. When I tell you who your Kindness Pal is I want you to say, 'Okay!' in a nice friendly way. Let's try that together!*

Are you always going to feel really excited about who you got? Maybe not. And that's okay. But how do you think we will make our Kindness pal feel if we say, 'Aw!' or, 'Rats!' or, 'But I wanted Lily!' That's right, they'll feel really bad. Since this is your Kindness Pal, it's your job to be kind to them - just for one day. So, the first kind thing you're going to do for them is to say, "Okay!"

Watch Intro to Kindness Pals Video (in slides)

Assign Kindness Pals
Remind the students to say, "Okay!". You can make a list ahead of time or put their names on popsicle sticks and pull them randomly out of a jar. However you want to do it is fine. Just make sure that they get a different child each time **and** that they say, "Okay!"

Kindness Pal Activity: Commonalities
Now we're going to do an activity with your Kindness Pal. When I say "Go!" you're going to find your Kindness Pal and then I'm going to give you 30 seconds to find out how many things you have in common - how many things are the same about you. You can ask each other about foods you like, animals, colors, books, movies, toys, whatever!

Share

Who thinks they have the most things in common? Have everyone share one thing that they had in common with their Kindness Pal.

Now for the rest of the day see if you can find any more things you have in common and try to do some kind things for your Kindness Pal.

5. Optional

Four Square Breathing Coloring Sheet (follows lesson)

6. Closing

Let's take a moment to think about something kind you could do for your Kindness Pal today. You can close your eyes if you want to.
Wait.
Ask: *Who has an idea already of what you might do?* **Invite a few answers.**
Thanks for a great class, everyone!
Ring a bell or chime if you have one.

Extension: *Peace of Mind Core Curriculum for Grade 4&5 Lesson 1, Page 18, for more about mindfulness, mindful bodies and Kindness Pals.*

Four Square Breathing

teachpeaceofmind.org
Copyright Peace of Mind 2024

Lesson 2
Take Five Breathing

Slides 13-23

1. Introduction

You might say: *Today we are going to learn another mindfulness practice and review the one we learned last time. We're going to spend some time with our new Kindness Pal and we're also going to introduce something called the Mindfulness Helper. The Mindfulness Helper will get to help me lead the mindfulness practices that we'll learn in each lesson.*

2. Mindful Moment

Choose the Mindfulness Helper

From now on you will choose a student to be the Mindfulness Helper for each class. That student will come up front to sit or stand next to you and help you to lead a mindfulness practice. If you have a little bell or chime you can let the Mindfulness Helper ring it at the end of the mindfulness practice.

Review Four Square Breathing.
Ask if anybody remembers how to do Four Square Breathing.
Choose a Mindfulness Helper and ask them to lead it with your help.

Have the Mindfulness Helper say: *Let's get into our mindful bodies. Let's close our eyes or look down. Let's do Four Square Breathing.*

> **Note:** *It's important <u>not</u> to require students to close their eyes or sit in a particular way. As long as the students are not bothering each other they are fine.*

Then practice a few rounds of Four Square Breathing. Have the Mindfulness Helper ring a bell or chime if you have one - not necessary!

Learn a new mindfulness practice with Marleigh's little brother Mason called Take Five Breathing. **Watch the video**

Try Take Five Breathing with the class.

Discuss

Does breathing this way make you feel any different? Did Take Five Breathing help Mason? Have you ever been mad about having to clean up when you wanted to play? How could Take Five Breathing help you? How do you feel?

3. American Sign Language (ASL)

You might say: *Today we're going to learn how to say "sad" in ASL. How do you feel in your body when you are sad?*

Choose a few volunteers to demonstrate what "sad" looks like.

Let's watch a video of one of the Peace of Mind students showing us how to sign "sad." **(the video is in the slides)**

ASL Practice

Have everyone try to say "sad" in ASL. Point out that the sign for "sad" involves our faces, hand gestures and body motions. Ask them if the sign for "sad" matches the way that they feel when they are sad.

4. Kindness Pals

Assign New Kindness Pals. You can make a list ahead of time or put their names on popsicle sticks and pull them randomly out of a jar. However you want to do it is fine. Just make sure that they get a different child each time and that they say "Okay!".

You might say: *Remember, every class we're going to get a new Kindness Pal. Your Kindness Pal is somebody that you will get to know a little bit better and you get to do kind things for them. Then next time you'll get a new Kindness Pal. There's one important rule of Kindness Pals. Does anybody remember what it is? When I tell you who your Kindness Pal is, I want you to say "Okay!" in a nice friendly way.*

Kindness Pal Activity: Mirror Game
You might say: *Now we're going to do an activity with your Kindness Pal. When I say "Go!" you're going to find your Kindness Pal and you're going to play the Mirror Game.*

We're going to be moving mindfully and really focusing on what our Kindness Pal is doing. What do you think it means to move mindfully? **Invite a few answers.**

Moving mindfully just means to really pay attention to how your body is moving.

Choose a volunteer to demonstrate the Mirror Game with you.

You are going to take turns being the leader and doing slow movements with your body. Your Kindness Pal will try to be your reflection in the mirror and do the exact same movements. After one minute I will ask you to switch and the other person will be the leader.

5. **Optional drawing activities**
   - Take Five Breathing Coloring Sheet (follows lesson)
   - Trace your hand and decorate it to help you remember how to do Take Five Breathing (worksheet follows lesson).

6. **Closing**

   Let's take a moment to think about something kind you could do for your Kindness pal today. You can close your eyes if you want to.
   Wait.
   Ask: *Who has an idea already of what you might do?* **Invite a few answers.**
   Thanks for a great class, everyone!
   Ring a bell or chime if you have one.

   Extension: *Peace of Mind Core Curriculum for Grade 4&5: Lesson 1, page 23, for the Kindness Pal Challenge, another activity that helps build connections among students. Lesson 8, page 54, Flashlight Body Scan for another way to practice mindfulness of our bodies.*

Take Five Breathing

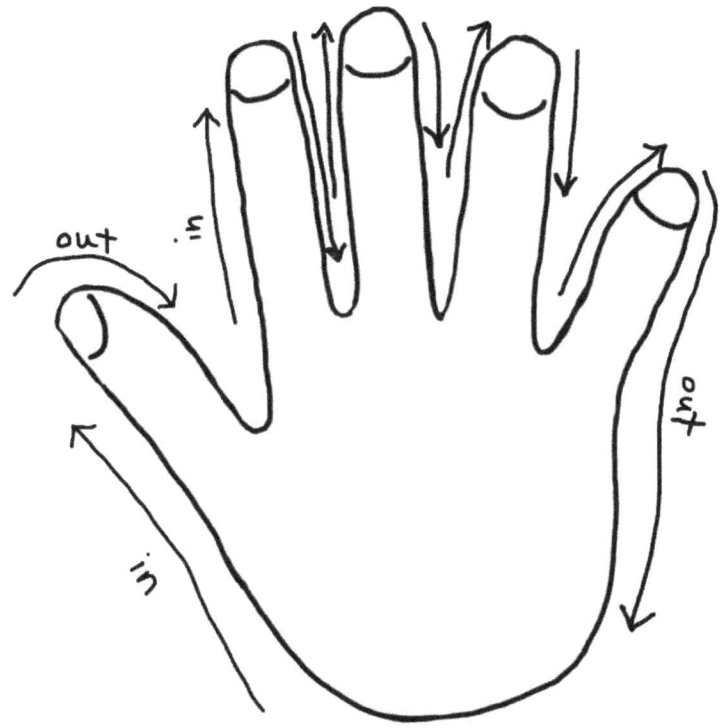

Slowly trace your hand breathing in as you
trace up and out as you trace down.

Take Five Breathing

Trace your hand and then decorate it to help you remember how to do Take Five Breathing.

Lesson 3
Gravity Hands

Slides 24-35

1. Introduction

You might say: *Today we are going to learn another mindfulness practice and review the one we learned last time. We're also going to talk about food with our Kindness Pals.*

2. Mindful Moment

Choose a Mindfulness Helper and Review

Ask if anybody remembers how to do Take Five Breathing.

Choose the Mindfulness Helper and have them lead Take Five Breathing.

Remind the MH to say, "*Let's get into our mindful bodies. Let's close our eyes or look down* (it's important **not** to require students to close their eyes). *Let's do Take Five Breathing.*"

Practice a few rounds of Take Five Breathing.

Ring a bell or chime (or let the Mindfulness Helper ring it) if you have one - not necessary!

Learn a new mindfulness practice with Navaneet called **Gravity Hands**. **Watch the video**. **Try** Gravity Hands with the class.

Discuss
Does breathing this way make you feel any different? How did Gravity Hands help Navaneet? Why do you think we call it Gravity Hands? How do you feel?

3. American Sign Language (ASL)

You might say: *Today we're going to learn how to say "angry" in ASL. How do you feel in your body when you are angry?*

Choose a few volunteers to demonstrate what "angry" looks like.

Let's watch a video of one of the Peace of Mind students showing us how to sign "angry." **(the video is in the slides)**

ASL Practice

Have everyone try to say "angry" in ASL. Point out that the sign for "angry" involves our faces, hand gestures and body motions. Ask them if the sign for "angry" matches the way that they feel when they are angry.

4. Kindness Pals

Assign New Kindness Pals. You might say: *It's time to get our new Kindness Pals! There's one important rule of Kindness Pals. Does anybody remember what it is? When I tell you who your Kindness Pal is I want you to say "Okay!" in a nice friendly way.*

Kindness Pal Activity: Food!
You might say: *When I say go, you're going to find your Kindness Pal and you're going to talk about food! Ask each other what is one of your favorite things to eat for breakfast, lunch, dinner and dessert. You've got one minute! Go!*

Share: *Now you're going to vote with your feet. This corner is for people who like sweet foods the best. The other corner is for people who like salty foods the best. Ready? Go!*

5. Optional

Gravity Hands Coloring Sheet (follows lesson)

6. Closing

Let's take a moment to think about something kind you could do for your Kindness pal today. You can close your eyes if you want to.
Wait. Ask: *Who has an idea already of what you might do?* ***Invite a few answers.***
Thanks for a great class, everyone!
Ring a bell or chime if you have one.

Extension: *Peace of Mind Core Curriculum for Grades 4&5: Lesson 4, Page 33. Try the See, Hear, Feel practice for another way to tune into our bodies during mindfulness practice.*

Gravity Hands

Slowly move your hands up
and down as you breathe in
and out.

Lesson 4
Flower Breathing

**Slides 36-46**

1. Introduction

You might say: _Today we are going to learn another mindfulness practice and review the one we learned last time. We're going to spend some time with our new Kindness Pal playing a game called "Switcheroo!"_

2. Mindful Moment

Choose a Mindfulness Helper and Review

Ask if anybody remembers how to do Gravity Hands.

Choose the Mindfulness Helper and have them lead Gravity Hands.

Remind them to say, _Let's get into our mindful bodies. Let's close our eyes or look down_ (it's important not to require students to close their eyes). _Let's do Gravity Hands._

Practice a few rounds of Gravity Hands. **Ring** a bell or chime if you have one.

Ask if anybody remembers how to do the other practices you've been learning. Ask them to demonstrate briefly.

Learn a new mindfulness practice with Josie and Cybbie called **Flower Breathing. Watch the video. Try** Flower Breathing with the class.

Discuss

How does Flower Breathing make you feel? How did Flower Breathing help Josie?

3. American Sign Language (ASL)

You might say: _Today we're going to learn how to say "scared" in ASL. How do you feel in your body when you feel scared?_

Choose a few volunteers to demonstrate what "scared" looks like.

Let's watch a video of one of the Peace of Mind students showing us how to sign "scared." **(the video is in the slides)**

ASL Practice

Have everyone try to say "scared" in ASL. Point out that the sign for "scared" involves our faces, hand gestures and body motions. Ask them if the sign for "scared" matches the way that they feel when they are scared.

4. Kindness Pals

Assign New Kindness Pals: Remind the students to say "Okay!" and make sure everyone is getting someone new today.

You might say: *It's time to get our new Kindness Pals! There's one important rule of Kindness Pals. Does anybody remember what it is? When I tell you who your Kindness Pal is, I want you to say "Okay!" in a nice friendly way.*

Kindness Pal Activity: Switcheroo

You might say: *When I say go, you're going to find your Kindness Pal and play Switcheroo!*

Choose a volunteer to model how to play the game.

You and your partner will observe each other for one minute, then turn your backs to each other and switch one thing. Turn around and take turns guessing what has changed about their partner. Ready? Go!

Ideas: Change your hair a little bit, roll down or up your sleeve, untie your shoe, pull up your sock. If they seem ready, you can up the challenge by changing **two** things.

5. Optional

Flower Breathing Coloring Sheet (follows lesson)

6. Closing

Let's take a moment to think about something kind you could do for your Kindness pal today. You can close your eyes if you want to.

Wait. Ask: *Who has an idea already of what you might do?*

Invite a few answers.

Thanks for a great class, everyone!

Ring a bell or chime if you have one.

Extensions: *Peace of Mind Core Curriculum for Grades 4 & 5: Lesson 7, page 48, The Finding Your Feelings Story to help students notice where they feel emotions in their bodies.*

Flower Breaths

Imagine you have a flower.
Smell the flower for four counts.
Blow the petals for four counts.

Lesson 5
Visualization

Slides 47-58

1. Introduction

You might say: *Today we are going to learn a different kind of mindfulness practice and review the one we learned last time. Instead of focusing on Mindful Breathing, we're going to be using our imaginations to travel to a Peaceful Place. Then we'll share about our Peaceful Place with our Kindness Pal and if we have time we'll draw a picture of it.*

2. Mindful Moment

Choose the Mindfulness Helper and Review
Ask if anybody remembers how to do Flower Breathing.
Choose the Mindfulness Helper and have them lead Flower Breathing.
Remind them to say, *"Let's get into our mindful bodies. Let's close our eyes or look down (it's important not to require students to close their eyes). Let's do Flower Breathing.* **Practice** a few rounds of Flower Breathing.
Ring a bell or chime if you have one.

Ask if anybody remembers how to do the other practices you've been learning. Ask them to demonstrate briefly.

Learn a new mindfulness practice with Malachi called Visualization.
Watch the video. **Try** Visualization with the class.

Discuss
Would Visualization help you fall asleep? Could it be helpful at other times?

3. American Sign Language (ASL)

You might say: *Today we're going to learn how to say "silly" in ASL. How do you feel in your body when you feel silly?*

Choose a few volunteers to demonstrate what "silly" looks like.

Let's watch a video of one of the Peace of Mind students showing us how to sign "silly." **(the video is in the slides)**

ASL Practice

Have everyone try to say "silly" in ASL. Point out that the sign involves our faces, hand gestures and body motions. Ask them if the sign matches the way that they feel when they feel silly.

4. Kindness Pals

Assign New Kindness Pals. You might say: *Okay it's time to get our new Kindness Pals! There's one important rule of Kindness Pals. Does anybody remember what it is? When I tell you who your Kindness Pal is I want you to say "Okay!" in a nice friendly way.*

Kindness Pal Activity: Sharing Peaceful Places
You might say: *When I say "go," you're going to find your Kindness Pal and take turns telling each other about what you visualized. What is in your peaceful place?*

Share: Give the class a chance to share about their Peaceful Place.

5. Optional

Visualization Coloring Sheet and Peaceful Place Drawing Sheet.

6. Closing

Let's take a moment to think about something kind you could do for your Kindness pal today. You can close your eyes if you want to.
Wait. Ask: *Who has an idea already of what you might do?* **Invite a few answers.**
Thanks for a great class, everyone!
Ring a bell or chime if you have one.

Extension: *Peace of Mind Core Curriculum for Grade 4&5, Lesson 5, p 38, Flashlight Body Scan.*

Draw a picture of your
Peaceful Place

What did you see, hear, smell, taste, touch, and feel?

Visualization

Imagine you are in a peaceful place.
Imagine what you would see, hear,
taste, smell and feel in that place.

Lesson 6
Make up Your Own Breath

Slides 59-67

1. Introduction

You might say: *Today we are going to make up our own way of doing mindful breathing and review the one we learned last time. You'll get to teach your idea to your Kindness Pal.*

2. Mindful Moment

Ask: *What has been your favorite mindfulness practice so far?* You could ask them to give you a thumbs up for the ones they like as you read off the list: Four Square, Take Five, Gravity Hands, Flower, or Visualization.

Choose the Mindfulness Helper

You might say: *Today the Mindfulness Helper gets to choose which breath we're going to do.*
Remind them to say, "*Let's get into our mindful bodies. Let's close our eyes or look down (*it's important not to require students to close their eyes*). Let's (*fill in with chosen practice) ….."*
Do the practice.
Ring a bell or chime if you have one.

3. American Sign Language (ASL)

You might say: *Today we're going to learn how to say "surprised" in ASL. How do you feel in your body when you feel surprised?*

Choose a few volunteers to demonstrate what "surprised" looks like.

Let's watch a video of one of the Peace of Mind students showing us how to sign "surprised" **(the video is in the slides)**

ASL Practice
Have everyone try to say "surprised" in ASL. Point out that the sign involves our faces, hand gestures and body motions. Ask them if the sign matches the way that they feel when they feel surprised.

4. Kindness Pals

Assign New Kindness Pals. You might say: *It's time to get our new Kindness Pals! There's one important rule of Kindness Pals. Does anybody remember what it is? When I tell you who your Kindness Pal is I want you to say "Okay!" in a nice friendly way.*

Kindness Pal Activity: Teach your own way of doing Mindful Breathing
You might say:*Today you're going to make up your own way of doing Mindful Breathing. It can be anything – Jellyfish Breath, Fireworks Breaths, Baseball Breaths — anything that lets you do simple, slow movements with three deep breaths. Then you'll teach it to your new Kindness Pal and then you're going to draw it. You're going to make a picture just like the ones we've been coloring in Peace Class.*

Invite students to draw their own mindful breathing practice on the attached worksheet and share their breath with their Kindness Pals. Invite students to share their ideas with the class.

5. Closing

Let's take a moment to think about something kind you could do for your Kindness pal today. You can close your eyes if you want to.
Wait.
Ask: *Who has an idea already of what you might do?* **Invite a few answers.**
Thanks for a great class, everyone!
Ring a bell or chime if you have one.

_____

Extension: Teach your new Mindfulness method to someone else and learn theirs.

Create Your Own
Mindful Breathing Practice!
My Mindful Breathing Practice is called:

_____

Lesson 7
Sergio Sees the Good

Slides 68-83

Note: For this lesson you will need some small paper cups and marbles, beans, beads, or something small; enough for every Kindness Pal Pair to have 3 cups and about 10 small objects.

1. Introduction

You might say: *Today's lesson will be a little different. I'm going to ask the Mindfulness Helper to choose one of the mindfulness practices we've learned, we'll learn some more ASL, and then we're going to listen to a story. We're going to learn about something called the Negativity Bias and then we're going to do a fun activity with our Kindness Pals.*

2. Mindful Moment

Choose Mindfulness Helper.

Let the mindfulness helper choose and help you to lead a mindfulness practice from all the practices you have learned so far.

Remind them to say, *"Let's get into our mindful bodies. Let's close our eyes or look down (it's important not to require kids to close their eyes). Let's (fill in with chosen practice)….."*

Ring a bell or chime if you have one.

3. American Sign Language (ASL)

You might say: *Today we're going to learn how to say "I feel" in ASL. Then we can start to say "I feel happy or I feel sad, etc."*

Let's watch a video of one of the Peace of Mind students showing us how to sign "I feel." **(the video is in the slides)**

ASL Practice

Have everyone try to say "I feel" in ASL. Then try adding some of the feeling words you've learned so far.

4. Gratitude and the Brain's Negativity Bias

Read the book or watch the video of <u>Sergio Sees the Good</u> (8 mins) OR if you don't have time you can watch this 4 minute video <u>Marleigh Sees the Good.</u> .

Discuss

- Do you remember what each marble represents?

- If all of the small objects are the same size, you might ask whether all of the things that Sergio (or Marleigh) remembered had the same "weight" or "size". Is waking up in a nice warm bed the same as hearing a funny joke?

- Do we sometimes forget about those big things and take them for granted?

- Have you ever had a day that was totally ruined? Looking back, do you think that was really true?

- What is the Negativity Bias?

- Do you think our Negativity Bias helps us in any way? (Cactus example)

- Does our Negativity Bias hurt us in any way?

5. Kindness Pals

Assign New Kindness Pals. You might say: *Okay it's time to get our new Kindness Pals! There's one important rule of Kindness Pals. Does anybody remember what it is? When I tell you who your Kindness Pal is I want you to say "Okay!" in a nice friendly way.*

Kindness Pal Activity: The Marble Game

Play the Marble Game.
Directions:

- Give each pair of Kindness Pals 3 paper cups and about ten marbles or other small objects. One cup is the "good" cup, one is the "bad" cup, and the other cup holds the small objects.

- Have them take turns.

- One student starts to recount their day to the other student. "I got up but I didn't want to. I put on my favorite shirt. I smelled waffles…"

- The student who's talking identifies each part of their day as good or bad. The student who is listening puts the marbles in the good or bad cups accordingly.

- Have students notice how many marbles are in each cup when all 10 have been used: what kind of day has it really been so far for that student?
- Then they pour the marbles out and switch.

> *Important Note:* *It's important to remind students that bad things sometimes happen and we're not trying to pretend that they don't. But our brains don't need help remembering those things. Our brains* <u>*do*</u> *need help remembering the good things, especially the little ones. So taming the Negativity Bias is a good way of helping us to see our lives as they really are - the good and the bad and not just the bad.*

6. Optional

Work on Sergio's Scales Coloring Sheet with their Kindness Pals

7. Closing

Let's take a moment to think about something kind you could do for your Kindness pal today. You can close your eyes if you want to.
Wait.
Ask: *Who has an idea already of what you might do?* ***Invite a few answers.***
Thanks for a great class, everyone!
Ring a bell or chime if you have one.

_____

Extension: *See the back pages in the book* <u>Sergio Sees the Good</u> *for more about the Negativity Bias and additional gratitude related activities.*

Sergio's Scale

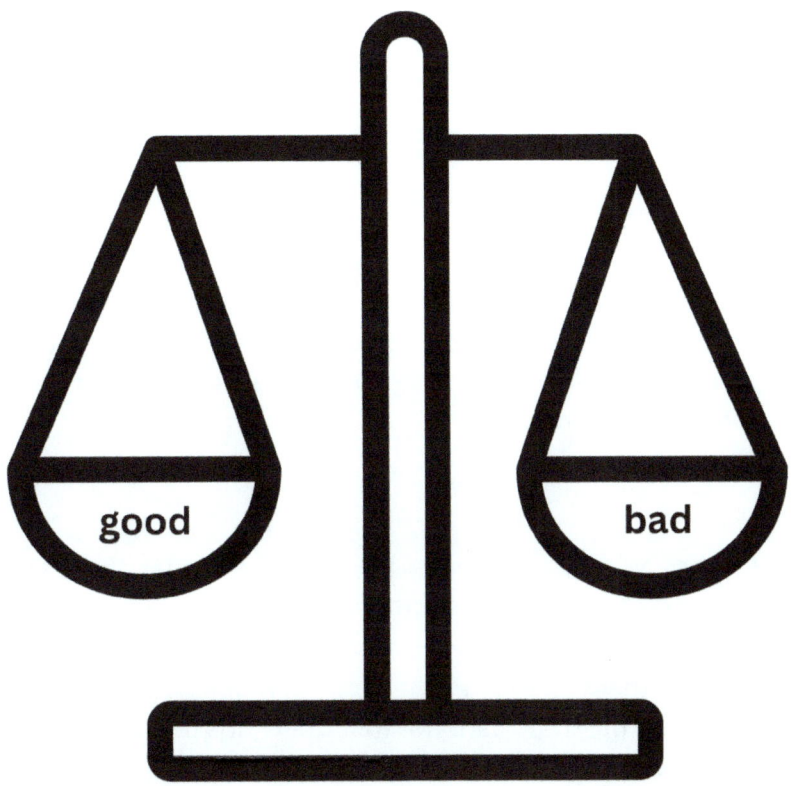

good   bad

Share with your Kindness Pal all the little things that
happened today and draw a marble on the good
side or the bad side for each thing you remember.

Lesson 8
Tell Me Something Good

Slides 84-92

__Note__: Before you teach this lesson you can listen to a little bit of this great old song by Chaka Khan. You'll just be singing the chorus. Tell Me Something Good You can start listening at 1:03. **Do not play the whole song for the class** *- it's not elementary school appropriate!*

1. Introduction

You might say: *Today I'm going to ask the Mindfulness Helper to choose one of the mindfulness practices we've learned and then we're going to play a game all together. Then you're going to make a list of little good things with your Kindness Pals.*

2. Mindful Moment

Choose Mindfulness Helper. **Let the mindfulness helper choose** and help you to lead a mindfulness practice from all the practices you have learned so far.

Remind them to say, *"Let's get into our mindful bodies. Let's close our eyes or look down (it's important not to require kids to close their eyes). Let's (fill in with chosen practice) ….."*

Ring a bell or chime if you have one.

3. American Sign Language (ASL)

You might say: *Today we're going to learn how to say "frustrated" in ASL. How do you feel in your body when you feel frustrated?*

Choose a few volunteers to demonstrate what "frustrated" looks like.

Let's watch a video of one of the Peace of Mind students showing us how to sign "frustrated." **(the video is in the slides)**

ASL Practice
Have everyone try to say "frustrated" in ASL.

Gratitude and the Brain's Negativity Bias

Play the game Tell Me Something Good!

You might say: *Do you remember the Negativity Bias and how sometimes it can be easy to forget to notice the little good things in our lives? Today we're going to learn a way to hack our Negativity Bias by helping to train our brains to be grateful. And to make it even more fun, we are going to sing a little song about it. I'm going to ask you to think of a little good thing in your life. You'll raise your hand when you're ready. When I call on you, we'll all sing Tell Me Something Good! And then you will. Let's try it. I'll go first. Sing it with me: Tell Me Something Good! And I'll tell you that I had waffles for breakfast (insert your own little good thing here). Your turn!*

4. Kindness Pals

Assign New Kindness Pals. You might say: *It's time to get our new Kindness Pals! There's one important rule of Kindness Pals. Does anybody remember what it is? When I tell you who your Kindness Pal is I want you to say "Okay!" in a nice friendly way.*

Kindness Pal Activity: Ten Little Good Things

You might say: *Now we're going to do an activity with your Kindness Pal. When I say "Go!" you're going to find your Kindness Pal and you're going to make a list of Ten Little Good Things. These can be really small things like "when the syrup fills up every little square in the waffle", or "hearing a kitten purr," or "the sound of a bat hitting a baseball," or "opening a new box of cereal." After you and your Kindness Pal have come up with your list we'll share out.*

5. Closing

Let's take a moment to think about something kind you could do for your Kindness pal today. You can close your eyes if you want to. **Wait.** *Who has an idea of what you might do?* **Take a few answers.** *Thanks for a great class, everyone!* **Ring** *bell.*

Extension: *Peace of Mind Core Curriculum for Grade 4&5: Lesson 14, Page 84. Try the Web of Gratitude practice.*

Ten Little Good Things

Your Name: _____

1. _____

2. _____

3. _____

4. _____

5. _____

6. _____

7. _____

8. _____

9. _____

10. _____

Lesson 9
Rosie's Brain

Slides 93-103

1. Introduction

You might say: *Today I'm going to ask the Mindfulness Helper to choose one of the mindfulness practices we've learned and then we're going to listen to a story called Rosie's Brain. Then you and your new Kindness Pal are going to find out how much you have in common.*

2. Mindful Moment

Choose Mindfulness Helper. **Let the mindfulness helper choose** and lead a mindfulness practice from all the practices you have learned so far.

Remind them to say, "*Let's get into our mindful bodies. Let's close our eyes or look down (it's important not to require students to close their eyes). Let's (fill in with chosen practice) …..*" **Ring** a bell or chime if you have one.

3. American Sign Language (ASL)

You might say: *Today we're going to learn how to say "excited" in ASL. How do you feel in your body when you feel excited?*

Choose a few volunteers to demonstrate what "excited" looks like.

Let's watch a video of one of the Peace of Mind students showing us how to sign "excited." **(the video is in the slides)**

ASL Practice

Have everyone try to say "excited" in ASL. Does the sign for "excited" match the way your body feels when you feel excited?

4. Three Important Parts of the Brain

Read the book or watch the video of Watch Rosie's Brain OR if you don't have time you can watch this 4 min video called Marleigh's Brain.

Discuss
- Why was Rosie (or Marleigh) angry?
- What did her amygdala (Amy) want her to do?

- Was Amy's idea (smashing the piano) a good one?
- How did her Hippocampus (Miss Pickles) help her?
- How did her PFC help her?
- Can you think of another way to solve Rosie's problem?
- What parts of your brain do you think you used to answer these questions?

5. Kindness Pals

Assign New Kindness Pals. You might say: *It's time to get our new Kindness Pals! There's one important rule of Kindness Pals. Does anybody remember what it is? When I tell you who your Kindness Pal is I want you to say "Okay!" in a nice friendly way.*

Kindness Pal Activity: Commonalities
You might say: *When I say "Go!" you're going to find your Kindness Pal and then I'm going to give you 30 seconds to find out how many things you have in common. Ask each other about foods you like, animals, colors, books, movies, toys, whatever!*

Ask: *Who thinks they have the most things in common?* Have everyone share one thing that they had in common with their Kindness Pal.

6. Optional

Brain Coloring Sheet

7. Closing

Let's take a moment to think about something kind you could do for your Kindness pal today. You can close your eyes if you want to. **Wait.** *Who has an idea already of what you might do?* **Invite a few answers.** *Thanks for a great class, everyone!* **Ring** *a bell or chime.*

Extension: *The Peace of Mind Core Curriculum for Grades 4&5: Unit 5 Brain on Science includes 3 interactive lessons to help students learn more about their brains.*

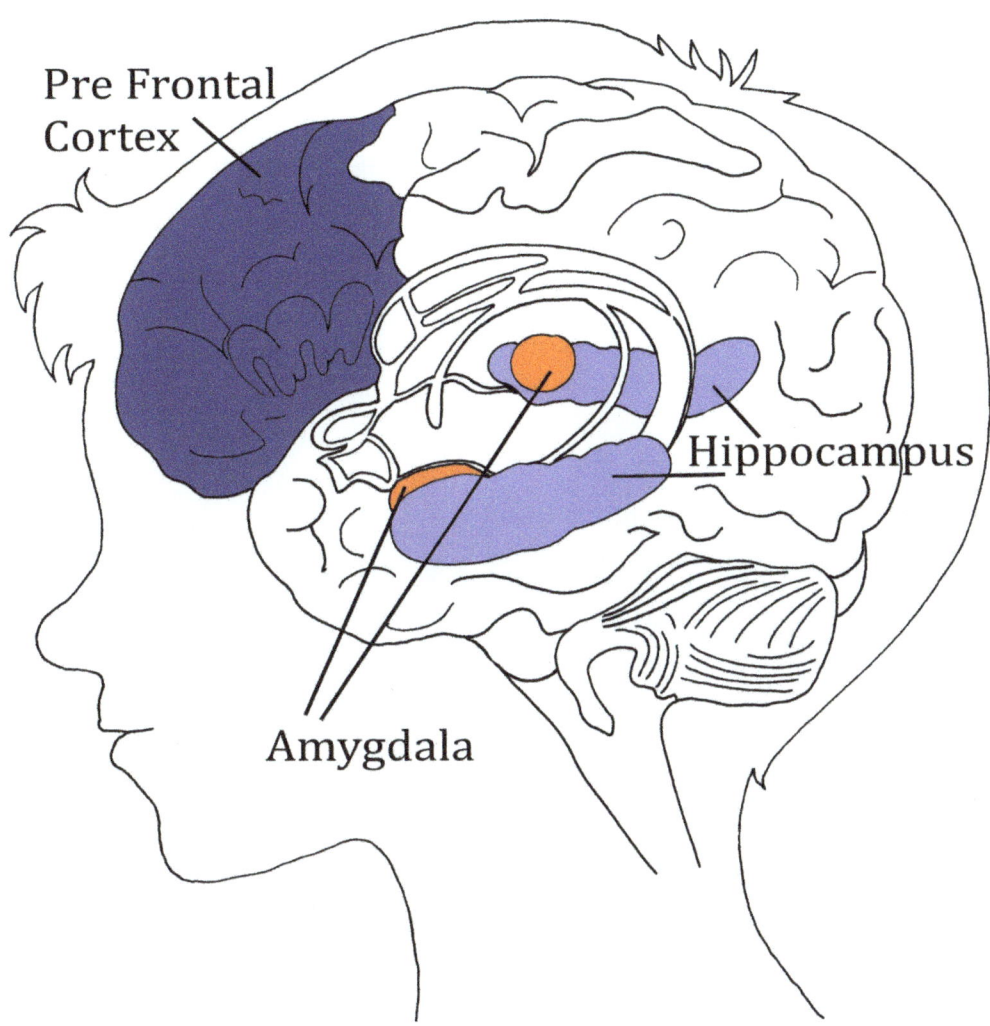

Pre Frontal Cortex

Hippocampus

Amygdala

Lesson 10
Mason and the Conflict CAT

Slides: 104-113

1. Introduction to the lesson

You might say: *Today we're going to do things a little differently and do our mindfulness practice after we read a story. The mindfulness practice for today will be taught in the story. Today we're going to read a book about conflict. It's called Mason and the Conflict CAT. What do you think the word "conflict" means? What do you think the Conflict CAT is? Does the cover of the book give you any clues?*

2. Conflict Resolution

Read the book or watch the video of Mason and the Conflict CAT.

Discuss

- What is a conflict?
- What was the conflict in the story?
- What made the conflict get better?
- Did some of the kids say things that made the conflict worse?
- Did all of the kids make the conflict bigger?
- What is the Conflict CAT? What do the letters stand for?
- How did the kids calm down?
- Why is it important to apologize?
- What were some of the tools in the Toolbox?
- What tool did the kids use to work out their conflict?
- Did everybody get exactly what they wanted?
- Is it okay if you don't get exactly what you want if you still get something pretty good?
- Do you ever have conflicts?
- How do you usually handle them?
- Could you imagine using the Conflict CAT?

3. Mindful Moment

You might say: Let's try Candle Breathing Now!
Choose Mindfulness Helper.

Remind them to say, *"Let's get into our mindful bodies. Let's close our eyes or look down (it's important not to require students to close their eyes). Let's try Candle Breathing."* Help them lead the practice.

Ring a bell or chime if you have one.

4. American Sign Language (ASL)

You might say: *Today we're going to learn how to say "How are you feeling today?" in ASL. Then we'll be able to ask each other about how we are feeling and answer!*

Let's watch a video of some Peace of Mind students showing us how to sign "How are you feeling today?." **(the video is in the slides)**

ASL Practice

Have everyone try to say "How are you feeling today?" in ASL.

5. Kindness Pals

Assign New Kindness Pals. You might say: *It's time to get our new Kindness Pals! There's one important rule of Kindness Pals. Does anybody remember what it is? When I tell you who your Kindness Pal is I want you to say "Okay!" in a nice friendly way.*

Kindness Pal Activity: Conflict Resolution Sharing
You might say: *When I say "go!" you're going to find your Kindness Pal and share a time that you have been in a conflict. How did you solve it?*

Invite a few pairs to share out.

6. Optional

Candle Breathing Coloring Sheet

7. Closing

Let's take a moment to think about something kind you could do for your Kindness pal today. You can close your eyes if you want to. **Wait.** *Who has an idea already of what you might do?* ***Invite a few answers.***
Thanks for a great class, everyone! **Ring** a bell or chime.

_____

Extension: *Peace of Mind Core Curriculum for Grades 4&5: Unit 6 includes 6 full lessons on Conflict Resolution.*

Lesson 11
Practice Using the Conflict CAT

Slides: 114-125

1. Introduction

You might say: *Today I'm going to ask the Mindfulness Helper to choose our mindfulness practice and then we're going to work with our Kindness Pals to practice using the Conflict CAT.*

2. Mindful Moment

Let the mindfulness helper choose and help you to lead a mindfulness practice from all the practices you have learned so far.

Remind them to say, *"Let's get into our mindful bodies. Let's close our eyes or look down (it's important not to require kids to close their eyes). Let's ….."*

Ring a bell or chime if you have one.

3. American Sign Language (ASL)

You might say: *Today we're going to learn how to say "hungry" in ASL. How do you feel in your body when you are hungry?*

Let's watch a video of some Peace of Mind students showing us how to sign "hungry." **(the video is in the slides)**

ASL Practice
Have everyone try to say "hungry" in ASL.

4. Conflict Resolution

Review the Conflict CAT
Ask:

- Who remembers what the letters CAT stand for in the Conflict CAT?
- What was the conflict that Mason and his friends had?
- Who can remember some of the tools in the Conflict Toolbox?
- What tool did Mason and his friends use to work out their conflict?

Practice using the Conflict CAT

You might say: *Today you get to be like Mason and his friends and see what it's like to use the Conflict CAT by doing something called role plays. I'll choose somebody to role play a conflict with me and we'll see what it feels like to use the Conflict CAT.*

Choose two students to act out a conflict. One will be Journey and one will be Jude. Journey and Jude are friends and always play together at recess. Today Journey wants to go outside and swing on the swings and Jude wants to stay inside and go to the Library.

Instructions to the two actors: *You're going to pretend that you are your character and you two are going to:*

- show the conflict escalating or getting bigger - just for a minute - don't get out of control;
- say "We're having a conflict;"
- say "Let's take some deep breaths;"
- apologize for whatever you did to make the conflict escalate;
- show us that you are using one of the tools in the Toolbox.

Discuss: So how did they do? Did you see all the steps of the Conflict CAT? Calm Down, Apologize, Toolbox? Now let's try it with our Kindness Pals.

5. Kindness Pals

Assign New Kindness Pals. You might say: *It's time to get our new Kindness Pals! There's one important rule of Kindness Pals. Does anybody remember what it is? When I tell you who your Kindness Pal is I want you to say "Okay!" in a nice friendly way.*

Kindness Pal Activity: Role Plays

You might say: *Now we're going to do an activity with your Kindness Pal. Today you're all going to get a chance to try a Conflict CAT role play with your Kindness Pal.*

Assign each pair a conflict scenario and ask them to act it out using the Conflict CAT

- You both want to check out the same book from the library.
- You want to play together but one of you wants to play basketball and the other one wants to play soccer.

- You want to play video games together but you can't agree on a game.
- You got a new guinea pig but you want to name it different names.
- You both want to sit in the special bean bag chair in your classroom.
- You're playing chess but you both want to go first.
- Choose another relevant scenario.

If you have time you could give a few pairs a chance to perform their role plays for the class.

6. Optional

Conflict CAT Coloring Sheet

7. Closing

Let's take a moment to think about something kind you could do for your Kindness pal today. You can close your eyes if you want to.
Wait. *Who has an idea of what you might do?* **Take a few answers.**
Thanks for a great class, everyone!

Extension: *Peace of Mind Core Curriculum for Grades 4&5: Unit 6 includes 6 full lessons on Conflict Resolution.*

The Conflict C.A.T.

Lesson 12
Quinn and the Worry Channel: Metacognition

Slides: 126-135

1. Introduction

You might say: *Today we're going to be learning about something completely different. We're going to be paying attention to our thoughts. We're going to read a story called Quinn and the Worry Channel and then we're going to spend some time working with our Kindness Pal. Our mindfulness practice will be taught in the story. But first let's learn some ASL!*

2. American Sign Language (ASL)

You might say: *Today we're going to learn how to say "thirsty" in ASL.* How do you feel in your body when you are thirsty?

Let's watch a video of some Peace of Mind students showing us how to sign "thirsty" **(the video is in the slides)**

ASL Practice
Have everyone try to say "thirsty" in ASL.

3. Metacognition

Read the book or Watch the Video of Quinn and the Worry Channel.

Discuss
- What is the Worry Channel?
- What was Quinn worrying about?
- Do you think most people worry?
- What did Fred the Bunny suggest that Quinn do to get his mind off of the Worry Channel?
- Is your mind on the Worry Channel sometimes?

4. Mindful Moment

Choose Mindfulness Helper.

You might say: *Let's try the mindfulness practice that is in <u>Quinn and the Worry Channel.</u> It's called Remote Control Breathing. First let's take a few deep breaths with Gravity Hands.*

Remind the Mindfulness Helper to say, *"Let's get into our mindful bodies. Let's close our eyes or look down (it's important not to require kids to close their eyes). Let's do Gravity Hands. And when we're done we'll stay in our Mindful Bodies to try Remote Control Breathing."*

You might say: *Now let's try to count our breaths. Imagine that you are setting your remote to the Counting Breaths Channel. For the next few moments just try to count your breaths and notice what happens. If you notice that your mind has wandered away that's fine. It's totally normal. Just see if you can try to change the channel back to the Counting Breaths channel. Let's try it.*

Leave about a minute for the class to try the exercise.

Ring a bell or chime if you have one.

Share

You might ask: *So what did you notice? Did your mind change the channel? Did your mind stay on the Counting Breaths channel? Was it tempting to stay on a different channel? Was it easy or hard to change the channel back? When could it be useful to redirect your focus?*
The more you practice this the easier and more helpful it gets!

5. Kindness Pals

Assign New Kindness Pals. You might say: *It's time to get our new Kindness Pals! There's one important rule of Kindness Pals. Does anybody remember what it is? When I tell you who your Kindness Pal is I want you to say "Okay!" in a nice friendly way.*

Kindness Pal Activity: What was on your Channel?
You might say: *When I say "go!" you're going to find your Kindness Pal and you're going to share about what channel your mind was on during the mindfulness practice. On the worksheet you can draw or write about the channels that you noticed.*

Invite a few pairs to share out.

6. Closing

"Let's take a moment to think about something kind you could do for your Kindness pal today. You can close your eyes if you want to."
Wait.
Who has an idea of what you might do? **Take a few answers.**
Thanks for a great class, everyone!
Ring a bell or chime if you have one.

—————————

Extension: *Peace of Mind Core Curriculum for Grades 4&5, Lesson 27, page 146 - Where are my Thoughts practice to help notice if we are focused in the past, present or future.*

Remote Control Breathing

Draw or write about a channel that your mind visited while you were trying to count your breaths.

teachpeaceofmind.org
Copyright Peace of Mind 2024

Lesson 13
Tyaja Uses the THiNK Test

**Slides: 136-145**

1. Introduction

You might say: _Today we're going to be thinking about how we talk to each other. Have you ever said something and then right away wished that you hadn't said it? That has probably happened to all of us. Today we're going to learn a little trick that can help us to think before we speak so we don't end up saying things that we later regret. I'm going to ask the Mindfulness Helper to choose a practice for us, we will learn a little more ASL, and later you'll get a chance to play a game with your Kindness Pal called Nine Words._

2. Mindful Moment

Let the mindfulness helper choose and help you to lead a mindfulness practice from all the practices you have learned so far.

Remind them to say, _"Let's get into our mindful bodies. Let's close our eyes or look down (it's important not to require kids to close their eyes). Let's ….."_

Ring a bell or chime if you have one.

3. Mindful Speaking

Read the book or watch the video of _Tyaja Uses the THiNK Test._

Discuss:

- What do the letters THNK stand for?
- What does the "I" stand for?
- How did the THINK Test help Tyaja?
- Why didn't she think she needed the THiNK Test?
- What's the difference between a need-to and a want-to?
- Are there times when you always need to use the THiNK Test?
- Are there times when you definitely don't need to use the THiNK Test?
- Can you think of a time when you wished you had used the THiNK Test?
- What does "words are like toothpaste" mean?

4. American Sign Language (ASL)

You might say: *Today we're going to learn how to say "peaceful" in ASL. How do you feel in your body when you are peaceful?*

Let's watch a video of some Peace of Mind students showing us how to sign "peaceful" **(the video is in the slides)**

ASL Practice
Have everyone try to say "peaceful" in ASL.

5. Kindness Pals

Assign New Kindness Pals. You might say: *It's time to get our new Kindness Pals! There's one important rule of Kindness Pals. Does anybody remember what it is? When I tell you who your Kindness Pal is I want you to say "Okay!" in a nice friendly way.*

Kindness Pal Activity: Nine Words
You might say: *When I say "Go!" you're going to find your Kindness Pal and play Nine Words. You're going to try to come up with nine words that start with the first letter of each one of your names. You need to think of three foods, three animals, and three of anything at all. For example, if my name is Linda and your name is Jeremiah, then we have to think of three foods that start with L and three foods that start with J, three animals that start with L and three animals that start with J, and then three of anything that start with L and with J. L: Linguine, Lollipops, Lettuce, J: Jam, Jelly, Jellybeans.*

6. Optional
THiNK Test Coloring Sheet

7. Closing

"Let's take a moment to think about something kind you could do for your Kindness pal today. You can close your eyes if you want to." **Wait.**
Who has an idea of what you might do? **Take a few answers.**
Thanks for a great class, everyone!
Ring a bell or chime if you have one.

___

Extension: *Peace of Mind Core Curriculum for Grades 4&5, Lesson 28, page 148, Fast and Slow thinking for more practice noticing our thoughts.*

Lesson 14
THiNK Test Role Plays

Slides: 146-156

1. Introduction

You might say: *Today we're going to practice using the THiNK Test. Who can remind us about the THiNK Test? What do those letters stand for? What does the "I" stand for? We're going to practice using the THiNK Test just like Tyaja. But first let's have a Mindful Moment. Later we'll find out how many things we have in common with our Kindness Pals.*

2. Mindful Moment

Let the mindfulness helper choose and help you to lead a mindfulness practice from all the practices you have learned so far.

Remind them to say, *"Let's get into our mindful bodies. Let's close our eyes or look down (it's important not to require kids to close their eyes). Let's ….."*

Ring a bell or chime if you have one.

3. American Sign Language (ASL)

You might say: *Today we're going to learn how to say "worried" in ASL. How do you feel in your body when you feel worried?*

Choose a few volunteers to demonstrate what "worried" looks like.

Let's watch a video of one of the Peace of Mind students showing us how to sign "worried" **(the video is in the slides)**

ASL Practice
Have everyone try to say "worried" in ASL. Point out that the sign involves our faces, hand gestures and body motions. Ask them if the sign matches the way that they feel when they feel worried.

4. Mindful Speaking

Watch the video of the THiNK Test activity

Try Using the THiNK Test

Choose 4 students to play the parts of the THiNK Test: Mr. True, Ms. Helpful, Ms. Necessary, and Ms. Kind. For the first few rounds the teacher can pose the challenge to the THiNK Test.

Challenge 1: *My birthday is coming up and I want to tell everybody in my class that I am having a birthday party at the bowling alley this weekend.*

Then ask Mr. True first. *"Mr. True, isn't it true that I am having a birthday party at the bowling alley this weekend?"* Mr. True can give a thumbs up or a thumbs down and then explain why they gave that answer. You can then ask the rest of the class to show a thumbs up or thumbs down and ask kids who agree with Mr. True and kids who disagree with Mr. True to share their thinking. Then repeat the process with Ms. Helpful, Mr. Necessary, and Ms. Kind.

Perhaps someone might wonder whether everyone in the class is invited to the party. Does that change the answer? Maybe only 5 kids can come to the party. Does that change the answer? Is announcing the party in class in front of everyone the only way to share this information? Are the kids who aren't invited going to be hurt?

> *Note: Remind your students that there is not necessarily only one right answer to these questions. The THINK Test is a tool to use to determine what YOU are going to do.*

Repeat with a new group of students and a new situation:
- You want to tell someone on your soccer team that they are not a good goalie.
- You want to tell everyone that you got the solo in the choir concert.
- You want to tell someone that you just overhead a girl telling her friend that she has a crush on Kyle.
- You want to tell someone that their favorite YouTuber is inappropriate.
- Discuss
- Do you think there are times when the THiNK Test could be really helpful?
- Do you think you always have to use the THiNK Test?
- Do you think the THiNK Test always tells you NOT to say something?
- Can you think of a time when the THiNK Test would say yes?

5. Kindness Pals

Assign New Kindness Pals as before.

Kindness Pal Activity: Commonalities
You might say: *When I say "go!" you're going to find your Kindness Pal and then I'm going to give you 30 seconds to find out how many things you have in common - how many things are the same about you. You can ask each other about foods you like, animals, colors, books, movies, toys, whatever!*

Who thinks they have the most things in common? Have everyone share one thing that they had in common with their Kindness Pal.

6. Closing

Let's take a moment to think about something kind you could do for your Kindness pal today. You can close your eyes if you want to. **Wait.**
Ask*: Who has an idea already of what you might do?* ***Take a few answers.***
Thanks for a great class, everyone! **Ring** a bell or chime if you have one.

|

Lesson 15
Kindness Taps

Slides: 157-167

1. Introduction

You might say: *Today is our last Peace of Mind session together. I've really enjoyed learning about mindfulness, brain science, conflict resolution and ASL with you. I hope you have enjoyed the class too! Today we're going to learn a different kind of mindfulness practice called Heartfulness. Heartfulness is kind of like an experiment - you see what it feels like to think kind things about people. You notice how it makes you feel. Scientists have shown that people who do this practice regularly are usually kinder to others and to themselves. Let's see what happens when we try it. Then we'll play a game all together.*

2. Mindful Moment

Watch the Jonah Heartfulness Video.

Remind the Mindfulness Helper one last time to say, *"Let's get into our mindful bodies. Let's close our eyes or look down (it's important not to require kids to close their eyes). Let's send kind thoughts to someone you care about who you've seen yesterday or today; to ourselves; to our whole class. May (you/I/ we all) be happy; May (you/I/we all) be healthy and strong; May (you/I/we/all) be peaceful. Take one more deep breath in and out.*

Ring a bell or chime if you have one.

Share: Ask if anyone wants to share what that felt like. Ask if anybody wants to share who they were sending their kind thoughts to.

3. American Sign Language (ASL)

You might say: *Today we're going to learn how to say "loved" in ASL. How do you feel in your body when you feel loved?*

Choose a few volunteers to demonstrate what "loved" looks like.

Let's watch a video of one of the Peace of Mind students showing us how to sign "loved". **(the video is in the slides)**

ASL Practice

Have everyone try to say "loved" in ASL. Point out that the sign involves our faces, hand gestures and body motions. Ask them if the sign matches the way that they feel when they feel loved.

4. Kindness Pals

Assign New Kindness Pals as before.

Kindness Pal Activity: Kindness Taps

This activity is designed to help children share the kindness they have been practicing in the previous 14 lessons in a new way.

Instructions:

Split your class in half. One half sits with their heads down and eyes closed (the sitters should sit evenly spread across the room so students aren't crowded together and others can walk around them). The other half stands in the back of the room (the standers).

The standers will walk around the room and gently tap students on the shoulder who they feel fit the identity of the person in the statements being read by the teacher. The teacher will read each of the following statements one at a time, giving 15-30 seconds after each statement to let the standers walk around and tap all the students they wish. Standers can tap any and all of the sitters. You can only tap more than one student per statement. During the walking/tapping time, the teacher is encouraged to monitor and tap students who they feel aren't getting as many taps as other students. The expectation is that students are doing this activity quietly.

Statements (feel free to add your own):

"This person makes me smile when I see them in the morning."
"This person has taught me something."
"This person has made me laugh or smile."
"This person has helped me feel better on a day I wasn't feeling my best."
"This person has pleasantly surprised me."
"I enjoy spending time with this person."
"I want to get to know this person better."
"I am grateful this person is in my class."
Switch sitters and standers. Repeat the exercise!

Discuss: What surprised you about what you got tapped for? What made you feel happy?

5. Closing

This is our last class together. I hope that you enjoyed learning more about mindfulness, kindness, and how to work out our conflicts peacefully. The world needs lots of kind, mindful people. Now you have some tools to help you go out into the world and make it a more peaceful place. I hope you will!

Thank you so much for a wonderful time together

Heartfulness

Who did you think your kind thoughts about?
Draw or write about them below.

May you be happy.
May you be healthy and strong.
May you be peaceful.

About Linda Ryden, Author

Linda Ryden is the author of seven mindfulness-based children's books published by Cherry Lake Publishing and Peace of Mind Inc. Linda is the founder and Creative Director of Peace of Mind Inc. and creator of the Peace of Mind Program and author of the Peace of Mind Curriculum Series, a cutting-edge combination of mindfulness-based social-emotional learning, conflict resolution and social justice for Early Childhood through Middle School. Linda served as the full-time Peace Teacher at Lafayette Elementary School, Washington DC's largest public elementary school from 2003 to 2023, teaching Peace of Mind classes to more than 700 students every week.

Linda's work has been featured in *The Washington Post*, *Washingtonian Magazine*, *Washington Parent*, *Washington Family*, *Teaching Tolerance*, and *Edutopia*, among others. Linda was a keynote speaker at the National Network of State Teachers of the Year conference and a featured speaker at the National Education Association Foundation Symposium, and has received a Commendation for Educational Innovation from the DC Board of Education.

Linda lives in Washington D.C. with her husband Jeremiah Cohen, owner of Bullfrog Bagels, and their dog Phoebe.

In that small but growing band of peace educators, Linda Ryden stands out. The glistening ideas and stories in these pages are sure to open minds and stir hearts, in much the way that has been happening all these years with the children in her classrooms.

— Colman McCarthy, Founder of The Center for Teaching Peace

Bibliography

Bradshaw, C. P. (2015). Translating research to practice in bullying prevention. American Psychologist, 70 (4), 322-332.

Breeding, K., & Harrison, J. (2007). Connected and Respected: Lessons from the Resolving Conflict Creatively Program. Cambridge, Mass.: Educators for Social Responsibility.

Durlak, J. A., Weissberg, R. P., Dymnicki, A. B., Taylor, R. D. & Schellinger, K. B. (2011). The impact of enhancing students' social and emotional learning: A meta-analysis of school-based universal interventions. Child Development, 82(1): 405–432.

Hanson, R. (2015). Hardwiring Happiness. Random House USA.

Jennings, P. (2015). Mindfulness for teachers: Simple skills for peace and productivity in the classroom. The Norton Series on the Social Neuroscience of Education.

Jennings, P. A. (2019). The Trauma-Sensitive Classroom: Building Resilience with Compassionate Teaching. New York: W.W. Norton & Company.

Lantieri, Linda. "How SEL and Mindfulness Can Work Together." Greater Good. April 7, 2015. Accessed September 28, 2015. http://greatergood.berkeley.edu/article/item/how_social_emotional_learning_and_mindfulness_can_work_together.

Learning Heroes, Developing Life Skills in Children: A Road Map for Communicating with Parents, https://bealearninghero.org/parent-mindsets/ September 2018

O'Brennan, L., & Bradshaw, C. (2013). School Climate: A Research Brief. A report prepared for the National Education Association, Washington, DC.

Rechtschaffen, D., & Kabat-Zinn PhD, J. (2014). The Way of Mindful Education: Cultivating Well-being in Teachers and Students. Norton Books in Education. Schonert-Reichl, K. A., & Lawlor, M. S. (2010). The effects of a mindfulness-based education program on pre-and early adolescents' well-being and social and emotional competence. Mindfulness, 1(3), 137-151.

Schonert-Reichl, K. A., Oberle, E., Lawlor, M. S., Abbott, D., Thomson, K., Oberlander, T. F., & Diamond, A. (2015). Enhancing cognitive and social–emotional development through a simple-to-administer mindfulness-based school program for elementary school children: A randomized controlled trial. Developmental Psychology, 51(1), 52-66.

Seppala, E., Simon-Thomas, E., Brown, S. L., Worline, M. C., Cameron, C. D., & Doty, J. R. (2017). The Oxford Handbook of Compassion Science. New York, NY: Oxford University Press.

Siegel, D. J., & Bryson, T. P. (2012). The Whole-Brain Child. London: Constable & Robinson.

Simmons, Dena (2019), Why We Can't Afford Whitewashed Social-Emotional Learning Retrieved from http://www.ascd.org/publications/newsletters/education_update/apr19/vol61/num04

Srinivasan, M. (2014). Teach, Breathe, Learn: Mindfulness in and out of the Classroom. Berkeley, CA: Parallax Press.

Treleaven, David (2018). Trauma-Sensitive Mindfulness: Practices for Safe and Transformative Healing. New York: W. W. Norton & Company.

Weare, K. (2013). Developing mindfulness with children and young people: A review of the evidence and policy context. Journal of Children's Services, 8(2), 141-153.

Zoogman, S., Goldberg, S.B., Hoyt, W.T., & Miller, L. (2015). Mindfulness interventions with youth: A meta-analysis. Mindfulness, 6, 290 - 302.

Zenner, C., Hermleben-Kurz, S., & Walach, H. (2014). Mindfulness-based interventions in schools: A systematic review and meta-analysis. Frontiers in Psychology, 5, article 603.

Appreciation

Peace of Mind is based in our community, and we are so lucky to have the support and guidance and help of so many wonderful people. We are grateful to Mike Di Marco, Valentina Gabrielli and the teachers and staff of Horizons Greater Washington for inspiring us to create this curriculum and being our first pilot program in summer 2024. A fantastic group of educators in the DC area and beyond piloted the Flex Curriculum during the 24-25 school year and provided helpful feedback. This curriculum wouldn't exist without many wonderful friends of Peace of Mind including Kelly Gilstrap, Jillian Diesner, Jodi Ferrier, Elie Goldman, Jennifer Greene, our friends at Metamer Studios, and the students who helped to create the amazing ASL and mindfulness videos. As always, we are able to do what we do at Peace of Mind thanks to the support of very generous foundations and kind individual donors! Thank you!!